4291 9786

SAVING THE BAGHDAD ZOO

A TRUE STORY OF HOPE AND HEROES

By Kelly Milner Halls with Major William Sumner

GREENWILLOW BOOKS

An Imprint of HarperCollins*Publishers*

For my dad, who taught me to love truth and animals—K. M. H.

For Heidi, who stayed home with a newborn daughter while I went off to war—W. S.

Front jacket image courtesy of U.S. Army (Staff Sergeant Joy Pariante, 13th Public Affairs Detachment)
Back jacket images: All photos courtesy of William Sumner except for bottom right, which is courtesy of
Spc. Chad D. Wilkerson, USA

Photos courtesy of William Sumner: Title page (all photos except tiger, peacock, puppy, and horse),
pages 8, 10 (left), 12, 13, 14, 15, 16, 17 (left), 19, 20, 21, 22, 23, 25, 26, 29, 30, 31, 32, 33, 34, 36, 37, 38,
39, 41 (top), 42, 43, 45, 46, 47, 48, 49, 50, 51, 56, 57, 58, 59, 61
Photos courtesy of U.S. Army:
   Title page (tiger), pages 54, 55: photos by Staff Sergeant Joy Pariante, 13th Public Affairs Detachment
   Pages 9, 10 (right), 40: photos by James Gordon, US Army Corps of Engineers
   Page 28 (right): photo by Sgt. 1st Class Kap Kim, USA
   Page 52: photo by Spc. Charles W. Gill, USA
Photo courtesy of Spc. Chad D. Wilkerson, USA: Title page (puppy)
Photo courtesy of Iraq Museum International: page 11
Photos © *The Washington Times* / Maya Alleruzzo, 2003: Title page (peacock), pages 4, 7, 17 (right), 35, 60
Photos © Micah Garen/Four Corners Media: Title page (horse), pages 18, 24, 27, 28 (left)
Photo © Arash Ghadishah/ABC News: page 41 (bottom)

Saving the Baghdad Zoo
A True Story of Hope and Heroes
Copyright © 2010 by Kelly Milner Halls and William Sumner
All rights reserved. Manufactured in China.
For information address HarperCollins Children's Books,
a division of HarperCollins Publishers, 10 East 53rd Street, New York, NY 10022.
www.harpercollinschildrens.com

Digital photography was used to prepare the full-color art.
The text type is Stempel Garamond.
Book design by Christy Hale

Library of Congress Cataloging-in-Publication Data

Halls, Kelly Milner, (date).
Saving the Baghdad Zoo : a true story of hope and heroes / by Kelly Milner Halls and William Sumner.
p. cm.
"Greenwillow Books."
Includes bibliographical references and index.
ISBN 978-0-06-177202-3 (trade bdg.) — ISBN 978-0-06-177200-9 (lib. bdg.)
1. Baghdad Zoo—Juvenile literature. 2. Zoo animals—Conservation—Iraq—Baghdad—Juvenile literature.
3. Wildlife rescue—Iraq—Baghdad—Juvenile literature. 4. Iraq War, 2003— I. Sumner, William, (date). II. Title.
QL76.5.I722B342 2009   590.73'56747—dc22   2008052820

09 10 11 12 13 LEO 10 9 8 7 6 5 4 3 2 1
First Edition

Greenwillow Books

INTRODUCTION

Major Henry Norcom escorting one of several unhappy goats from Luna Park. The park was a small zoo, located next to Martyr's Monument in eastern Baghdad.

I RECALL THINKING THAT THE TUNNEL we had entered would be a great place to set up an ambush. About that same time, I remember, someone from the rear of our convoy yelled, "Sniper!" and troops jumped from their vehicles to take up defensive positions. Major Henry Norcom, standing in the back of the lead vehicle, scanned the top of the bridge as he emerged into the daylight again. I flipped the safety off my weapon, leaned back, and told Brendan Whittington-Jones to watch our side for problems. I tried to take stock of the situation.

It was about this time that the sedative given to the striped hyena began to wear off and the swan in my backseat, being held in a bear hug by Dr. Barbara Maas, decided that it was a good time to be somewhere else.

We were removing a large number of animals from Luna Park, a decrepit little zoo where the animals were held in some of the unhealthiest conditions imaginable. As a result, my convoy was a rolling menagerie consisting of three agitated rhesus monkeys, a drowsy hyena, an angry swan, several pigs, a number of goats, three porcupines, a full-grown pelican, a collection of underfed dogs, and a camel named Lumpy, who was strapped down in the back of one of our troop carriers. Everyone was tense, and Lumpy was no longer amused by his personal tour through the heart of Baghdad, but on the bright side, at least, we had temporarily left the six hundred-pound brown bear at Luna Park, since our trucks were full.

Before I went to Iraq, I had a lot of ideas about what war would be like, but none of them proved to be right. I was deployed to Iraq as a civil affairs officer, trained as an archaeologist, to work with the Iraqis to restore their cultural heritage. Shortly after arriving there in April 2003, I was asked by the commander of the 4/64 Armor to look at a "small zoo" he had in his area. The "small zoo" turned out to be one of the largest zoos in the Middle East, plus three palace zoos and a number of other animal collections. I was amazed that the lions, tigers, and bears, among other animals, had survived the fighting and looting and now were mostly threatened by a lack of food and water. Critical machinery at the zoo, such as water pumps, had been destroyed; ammunition and other weapons were littered throughout the park; and everything of value had been looted after the fall of the city. The soldiers of the 3rd Infantry Division, who had fought against the Iraqis entrenched in the park, did their best to take care of the remaining animals. They even used their own supplies to provide food. But more needed to be done.

Throughout the next several weeks, the day-to-day crisis of finding

WHO IS WILLIAM SUMNER?

I'm Major William Sumner—Wes to my friends. I was born in Jacksonville, Florida, on June 10, 1971. I had three older brothers—much older. They were practically grown by the time I came along. So I kept myself busy reading books, playing soccer, and dreaming of the day I could join in a proud family tradition.

My grandfather had been a member of the United States armed forces when he was a young man; so had his father. I knew I would eventually follow in their footsteps. In fact, I trained for it in high school and college even before I stepped up to join.

I always wanted to be a pilot. But that didn't work out. I studied archaeology and education instead and was awarded my master's degree in both. But it was common sense, determination, and a love for animals that prepared me for a mission I never could have imagined: saving a war-torn zoo.

Why did I want to help write a book about this mission? I have a wife and two little girls, six-year-old Morgan Riley and three-year-old Sydney Paige. I liked the idea of sharing the story with them and with other kids all over the world.

food, getting replacement parts, and providing medical care to both the animals and the staff consumed everyone who became involved with the zoo. The recovery effort was a symbol of the international cooperation that I had been told to expect in Iraq but had not previously experienced. Iraqis, South Africans, Americans, and Britons all struggled together daily to provide basic amenities for the remaining animals. While explosions and gunfire rattled the city, we battled looters, insurgents, disease, shortages of food, water, and electricity, all while lacking even the most basic tools for taking care of the animals.

During my time in Iraq, I was asked repeatedly why we were helping the animals and not the people of Baghdad, but I believe that we were doing both. We were not only saving the animals; we were also helping the people who worked with them. We gave them jobs, fed their families, provided medical care, and forged friendships that last to this day. In some cases—for example, the recovery of sixteen Arabian horses—we preserved unique national symbols of the Arabic culture. We opened the surrounding park, which provided a green space in the heart of Baghdad that became a refuge from the day-to-day violence occurring in the city while at the same time improving living conditions for the animals in the zoo.

The stories contained in this book depict the efforts of a number of people to save the zoo, to help a large population of forgotten animals, and to protect the national heritage of Iraq. During my time in Baghdad, we experienced many daily challenges that were exacerbated by language barriers, supply shortages, disease, and the constant threat of attack from the insurgency. It was not unusual to hear explosions and fighting nearby while we worked, and threats against our lives and the lives of our staff were commonplace.

While I am pleased to share my story and the stories of others who worked to save the Baghdad Zoo, I encourage you to learn more about

Specialist Wirges distracting a monkey en route to the Baghdad Zoo.

the animals and understand the challenges we faced. If you take away one thing from this book, I hope it is that the zoo survived the conflict and now thrives because of the commitment and courage of a group of people who fought to keep the animals alive. Teddy Roosevelt once said, "Do what you can, with what you have, where you are." I like to believe that we did just that.

I hope you enjoy reading about the experience of saving the Baghdad Zoo because despite everything, I enjoyed living it.

—William Sumner

ONE
SHOCK AND AWE

ABOVE AND RIGHT: Buildings at Saddam Hussein's "Water Palace" destroyed during the initial days of the invasion. The palace, located adjacent to the main airport, is now called Camp Victory, and serves as one of the larger coalition bases in Iraq.

IT WAS APRIL 2003 IN IRAQ. THE WAR HAD LEFT THE capital city of Baghdad in tatters. Thousands of U.S. bombs had rained down on the city in less than a month—a wave of air strikes known as "shock and awe." Iraqi citizens were desperate. Food was scarce. Hunger showed on their faces. So did the grime and blood of war.

Enter Captain William Sumner of the U.S. Army 354th Civil Affairs Brigade. Trained in archaeology, he had been ordered to archive the priceless relics of the Baghdad Archaeological Museum (now known as the Iraq Museum International), ancient treasures up to seven thousand years old. He believed he would save and defend those antiquities. But his mission was about to change.

"There is a zoo in al-Zawra Park," Captain Sumner's commanding officer, Colonel William Sollenburger, said. "Why don't you go and

check it out?" Captain Sumner's expertise was not zoological. As an animal lover, he was happy to obey the order, but unprepared for what he was about to see.

Contrary to television and newspaper reports, the zoo had not been torn apart by stray explosives. Animals had not been killed by military fire or missiles. But only thirty-two of five hundred creatures once on display were still caged. Hundreds were missing, butchered for food or stolen for sale as exotic pets on the Iraqi black market. Even two giraffes, new residents delivered the day before the first bombs fell, had simply vanished.

ABOUT IRAQ AND THE IRAQ MUSEUM INTERNATIONAL

Today we call it Iraq. But for thousands of years, it was known by another name—Mesopotamia, "the land between two rivers." Iraq is bisected by the Tigris and Euphrates rivers. Babylon once thrived between their banks. Iraq has also been referred to as the Cradle of Civilization.

Evidence of the region's ancient history, including sculptures, pottery, jewelry, textiles, tablets, and more, was displayed in the Iraq Museum under the reign of Saddam Hussein. Before American bombs were dropped, thousands of treasures were moved to safer places or sandbagged for protection. But others were destroyed or stolen.

In April 2003, I began my first Iraqi mission, working with other experts to recover and archive the irreplaceable museum items for display in what is now known as the Iraq Museum International. Visit www.baghdadmuseum.org for a virtual look at what originally brought me to Iraq.

One of several Assyrian artifacts on exhibit in the Iraqi Museum International. This exhibit was not damaged during the invasion, thanks to the extraordinary efforts of the museum staff.

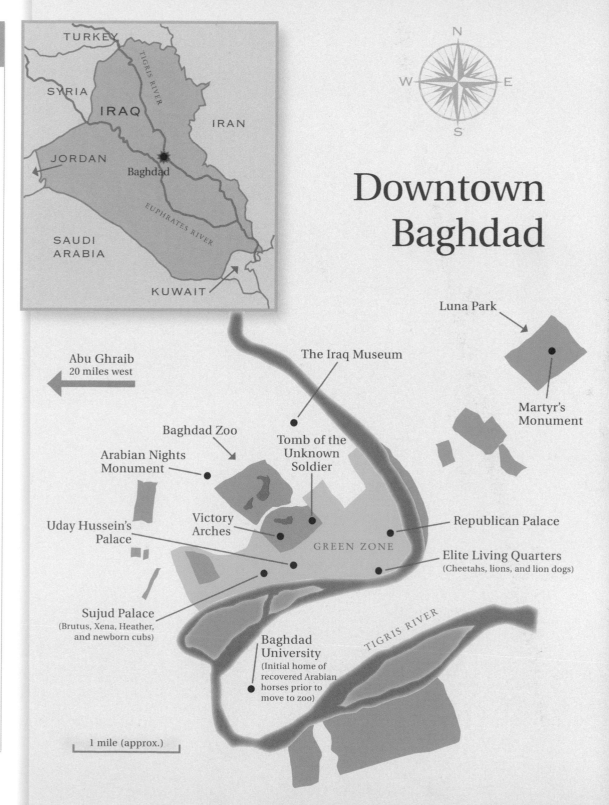

Downtown Baghdad

TURKEY
SYRIA
IRAQ
TIGRIS RIVER
IRAN
JORDAN
Baghdad
EUPHRATES RIVER
SAUDI ARABIA
KUWAIT

Abu Ghraib
20 miles west

Luna Park

The Iraq Museum

Martyr's Monument

Baghdad Zoo

Tomb of the Unknown Soldier

Arabian Nights Monument

Uday Hussein's Palace

Victory Arches

GREEN ZONE

Republican Palace

Elite Living Quarters
(Cheetahs, lions, and lion dogs)

Sujud Palace
(Brutus, Xena, Heather, and newborn cubs)

Baghdad University
(Initial home of recovered Arabian horses prior to move to zoo)

TIGRIS RIVER

1 mile (approx.)

TWO

FIRST THINGS FIRST

ABOVE: Prior to the war, these cages held exotic birds for visitors to enjoy. The animals were looted and most likely sold on the black market, or kept by the crowds that descended on the zoo after the invasion.

RIGHT: A Luna Park impala in need of immediate rescue. When we found the animals, they did not have water or food, and their cages were filled with garbage.

KEEPERS WHO ONCE CARED FOR THE ANIMALS AT THE Baghdad Zoo were forced to seek safe shelter as their homeland was transformed into a war zone. Animals locked in steel-and-concrete enclosures were not so lucky.

Captain Sumner's first step was to patrol the zoo and find out if any living thing could be saved. Volunteers soon appeared to offer assistance. Lawrence Anthony, a civilian conservationist from South Africa, arrived, followed by a young Iraqi veterinarian named Dr. Farah Murrani and by Brendan Whittington-Jones, another conservationist employed by Anthony on the Thula Thula Game Reserve.

They found that most of the cages were empty—torn open and stripped bare. Some animals had died of starvation. The scattered few that survived were fearsome. Ferocious by nature, too dangerous to

Once saving the Baghdad Zoo became a priority, making sure every animal was fed became the primary challenge. But as bombs fell and bullets flew, finding food for human beings was difficult. Finding the portions necessary to feed exotic creatures was almost impossible. What did the captive animals need to fill their bellies and move toward good health?

According to St. Louis Zoo animal nutritionist Dr. Ellen Dierenfeld, the answer to that question depends on many factors, including the age, size, climate, and activity levels of the animal in question. But she offered her expert opinion on these six species, based on what the average American zoo animal might eat under her watchful eye. Remember, these lists represent what each animal would typically eat *every single day* in captivity.

Brown bear Eats 7 pounds dry dog food, 2 pounds meat with added vitamins and minerals, 1.5 pounds whole fish or chicken.

Pelican Whole-fish–based diet with added vitamins B_1 (25 mg/kg fish) and E (50 IU/kg fish). Pelicans eat about 10 to 20 percent of their weight in food every day.

Camel Eats around 1 percent of body weight per day, good-quality grass hay, salt should be available, and a small portion of livestock pellets (no more than 25 percent of diet) could be added.

Ostrich Grazes and can successfully be fed grass hay, green plant materials, and herbivore pellets. Ostriches eat 1 to 2 percent of body weight daily.

Porcupine High-fiber biscuits, green plant materials, and root vegetables, such as sweet potatoes. Porcupines also love to chew on whole corn on the cob. Needs wood or something hard to keep teeth sharp and worn down properly, or teeth will misalign. Quantities: maybe 3 percent of body weight daily (fresh).

Bengal tiger Eats 5 to 8 pounds of meat with vitamin and mineral supplements. If the tiger is eating whole prey, with bones and organs consumed, there is less need for the supplements. Should be fed large bones one or two days per week to stimulate and clean teeth and gums.

steal, many were even more deadly after days without food.

Not long after the first appraisal of the zoo, Captain Sumner and his team evaluated Saddam Hussein's eldest son Uday's exotic animals, abandoned at Uday Hussein's residences, and the survivors at Luna Park, a smaller zoo in the Red Zone, the most dangerous part of town. Conditions at Luna Park were even worse than they were at the Baghdad Zoo. In fact, one expert recommended that all of the animals should be put down; they were too far gone to save.

Captain Sumner and his new companions

agreed the conditions were heartbreaking. But he wasn't willing to give up. He knew action, not tears, would give these animals a second chance. And he was determined to find a way.

Getting the animals fed was the team's first challenge. They struggled with it daily. Bombs had demolished public utilities, so running water was not an immediate possibility. Even simple things like buckets had been destroyed or stolen from the zoo. The volunteers filled anything that would hold liquid with water they scooped out of the nearby river.

Food was even harder to find. "We didn't know what the animals ate, at first," Captain Sumner explained, "so we were feeding them military issue MREs—'Meals Ready to Eat.'"

Calls to England's London Zoo, the world's oldest zoological park, and the North Carolina Zoo in Asheboro gave Captain Sumner a crash course in animal nutrition. But two pressing questions remained.

LEFT: Dr. Farah Murrani in front of a spice shop haggling for a better price. These markets (called suqs) are similar to grocery stores, except that most prices are subject to debate.

MIDDLE: A butcher shop in the local suq. Butchers in Baghdad let nothing go to waste.

ABOVE: Frozen bison meat to the rescue, thanks to Care for the Wild International and Dr. Barbara Maas. The search for working freezers came next.

Time spent in a land torn apart by war is never easy. Each moment could be the last for soldiers far from home or for civilians in their own backyard. Each moment is filled with tension. An unexpected sound could be a sign of danger. Is it any wonder a steady stream of people wanted to help at the zoo?

"We never had a shortage of volunteers," Captain Sumner said. "I'd say, 'There is a mission that involves the zoo,' and people would line up to help. At the zoo, they could help animals and do things they would not normally be able to do. At the zoo, we were really making a difference."

Dozens of able-bodied troops, Iraqi citizens, and global rescue workers stepped up to do their part, and you'll read about some of them in this book. Even a group of the original Baghdad Zoo staffers soon made their way back to the zoo. But a few unwavering regulars stood shoulder to shoulder with Captain Sumner.

Dr. Farah Murrani arrived just days after Captain Sumner took on the mission, asking to work even if she wouldn't be paid. She went to the zoo because of her love for animals.

Brendan Whittington-Jones, a wildlife zoologist, came to join his boss, Lawrence Anthony, from the Thula Thula Game Reserve in South Africa. They were some of the first non-Iraqi civilians willing to help.

U.S. Army veterinary technician Erin McLoughlin from the Coalition Joint Task Force 7's 72nd Medical Detachment—and Michigan, back at home—went to work against overwhelming odds.

Time and again, these individuals and others worked with Captain Sumner to bring the impossible within reach. They proved how powerful people can be when they join forces. They proved they could make a difference.

Dr. Farah Murrani with one of our rescued dogs. She helped to ship more than forty animals, adopted by soldiers, to new homes in the United States.

Specialist Erin McLoughlin working to help one of the many large birds that were returned to the Baghdad Zoo after the looting ended.

LEFT: When frozen meat was unavailable, carnivores still had to eat. Donkeys were a nutritional alternative.

BELOW: Captain Sumner holding one of several dogs rescued from the Luna Park zoo.

Where would they get the food? And who would pay the bills?

"Sometimes we simply begged," Captain Sumner said. Other times they'd get more creative. When one of the captain's superior officers found a cache of rye, a grain used to make bread, it was sold to pay for animal food.

If begging and bartering failed, Captain Sumner, his team, and the volunteers spent money of their own. "What else could we do?" he said. "They were like our kids. If we didn't take care of the animals, who would?"

Eventually relief organizations such as the North Carolina Zoological Society, the International Fund for Animal Welfare (IFAW), and WildAid heard about the effort and offered to help. And the U.S. Army funded aid whenever it could. But thanks to Captain Sumner's strongest allies—including the three you'll see featured in this book—feeding the animals got a little easier. With that problem under control, bigger challenges demanded their attention.

THREE
HARD TO BEAR

ABOVE: "Last Man Standing" in his roomier new enclosure at the Baghdad Zoo.

RIGHT: Saedia enjoying a snack. Fruits and vegetables helped keep her healthy.

Families caught in the crossfire between warring armies live in fear, no matter what side of the struggle they are on. The sound and smell of gunfire just blocks or footsteps away, the rumble of tanks rolling down their hometown streets, or the rain of artillery can force a family to pack up and move away.

Saedia, the thirty-two-year-old brown bear at the Baghdad Zoo, didn't have that option. As destruction fell from the sky, Saedia, who is blind, couldn't run, as her instincts told her to do. One of her Iraqi caretakers, Dr. Husham Mohamed Hussan—one of the first to return to the zoo—took some comfort in thinking, At least she can't see the bombs. But she couldn't even sniff out water when the tiny trough in her twenty-by-twenty-foot enclosure ran dry.

Why did it run dry? Electric pumps were programmed to maintain

In North America and parts of Europe, brown bears live naturally in the heavily forested wilderness. But in Iraq, brown bears are exotic and rare, and found only in traveling circuses and zoos. Visitors travel for miles just to capture a glimpse of them. These fast facts will tell you what they find, once they do.

Scientific name: *Ursus arctos*

Adult size: 5½ to 10 feet long

Adult weight: 200 to 1,500 pounds

Coloration: Blond, brown, black, or a combination of the three

Normal diet: Omnivorous—vegetables and meat (fish and small mammals)

Little-known facts: The brown bear can run up to 35 miles per hour and is the national animal of Finland. Its rear pawprints are sometimes mistaken for the tracks of the legendary Bigfoot.

the zoo's entire watering system. But when Baghdad's utility companies became disabled, the citywide electrical system shut down. No electricity, no pump. No pump, no water. In a matter of days, the troughs ran dry, and no one was left to fill them.

All Saedia could do was pace, growl, and rub her head against immovable green metal bars. Back and forth she ambled. She bruised her paws against the concrete. She displayed all the signs of an animal in distress.

Like Saedia, Specialist Erin McLoughlin had felt the weight of the war's ominous firepower. "She'd come pretty close to losing her life in a shelling incident," Captain Sumner explained. "So she understood. She was very eager and well qualified to help."

Specialist McLoughlin and Coalition Joint Task Force 7 veterinarian Colonel Mark E. Gants heard about Saedia and swiftly came to her rescue. But eight-foot-tall, frightened bears that tip the scales at more than 500 pounds (even when they're starving) don't always know the difference between friends and foes. So the first step was to dart the bear with rifle-fired sedatives, to put her to sleep temporarily.

With steady aim, Colonel Gants delivered the drugs, and in minutes, the examination had begun. Stress and malnutrition were not Saedia's only problems. Her claws had grown so long she was in pain with

FAR LEFT: Baghdad Zoo director Dr. Adel Salman Mousa and Specialist Erin McLoughlin ready the tranquilizer darts for Saedia.

LEFT: Brendan Whittington-Jones trimming Saedia's claws with a Leatherman tool. All of the zoo's proper tools had been stolen, so we had to use whatever we could find or improvise in order to take care of the animals.

every step she took. She had cataracts in both of her eyes, which confirmed she was visually impaired. And she had a tumor on her chest.

"When you have a malignant tumor," Specialist McLoughlin reported in a Department of Defense article, "it's not good. You need to get it out of there. . . you want to prevent it from spreading."

With gentle hands, she shaved Saedia's tender belly and helped Colonel Gants cut the tumor away. They disinfected the wound, gave Saedia antibiotic injections to fight further infection, and carefully stitched her up. Then, as the vulnerable bear snoozed, they cut and filed back her overgrown claws with Captain Sumner's Leatherman tool and treated the pads of her feet.

When Saedia's sedatives wore off, her surgical team was not only happy but relieved. She would recover, and with her tumor gone, she had a good chance of living the rest of her life—three to five years at most—in a far safer home. But Brendan Whittington-Jones decided five more years in a concrete cell wouldn't do. Saedia would enjoy a home makeover.

With modest funding from the U.S. Army, the team fenced in the grassy scrap of land behind the existing bear enclosure. Using an old sledgehammer, they broke open a hole in the cage wall. When the barrier between Saedia and the natural world came down, the blind bear "shot outside," Captain Sumner said. "She could apparently see light," he continued, "and she could probably smell the grass.

"It was the first time she had ever felt grass beneath her feet," Captain Sumner said. And once outside she just lay down and didn't move. In fact, she didn't go back inside her enclosure for days. With the gift of a tiny patch of land, Saedia's world had been greatly expanded.

Saedia enjoying a meal of bread and fruit during her first day outside of her enclosure.

The bear had been there for twenty-three years in the same twenty-by-twenty-foot enclosure. It was very small, and had a concrete-pad floor, a concrete water bowl, a small set of bars, and another small set of bars in the back to let additional light in, and that was it. The director, Dr. Adel Salman Mousa, said the bear had always been there. As long as he had been there, the bear had been there. It was assumed the bear was blind. We found out later she just had bad cataracts.

She looked miserable. She sat in one corner of her enclosure and didn't move. We tried to feed her and get her things that would amuse her, but it just didn't take. Colonel Mark E. Gants and Specialist Erin McLoughlin cleaned her up, trimmed her claws, which apparently had never been done, cleaned her ears. We found a tumor on her chest as well, and Colonel Gants removed it.

Specialist McLoughlin checks on Saedia, who later made a full recovery.

It was amazing that she had been living in these conditions for so long and had never had known anything else, so she was one of our special projects. She stayed out back in the grass, walking around, for months. She never went into her cage, except for one or two times to get food. It was one of the happier things I'd seen, because you know at that point, you've made a difference. You could tell she was happy.

When one of our nongovernmental organization representatives, Dr. Barbara Maas, tried to have her flown to a bear reserve in Greece, we had one of our first protests at the zoo, which I thought was amazing. All these Iraqi people had been under Saddam for so long, and if you spoke out against him, chances were good you'd be taken away in the night. But when Dr. Maas tried to take the bear, the workers came out with their own signs and picketed—said they didn't want their animals and heritage taken.

It was a spontaneous demonstration of free expression that showed we were making progress and were on the right track. It showed how far we'd come, cooperating with the zoo workers, taking care of them as well as the animals; we were giving them a sense of empowerment, becoming a team. The bear was a rallying point for them, and it was an amazing thing to have happened.

For brown bear Saedia, things were looking up at the Baghdad Zoo. But across town at Luna Park, Samir—or, as Lawrence Anthony called him, "Last Man Standing"—was still in grave danger.

Baghdad is not a tiny village. It is the second-largest city in the Middle East, and it once teemed with more than seven million people. Like many urban centers, Baghdad had a large zoo funded by the government and other small petting zoos owned by private citizens. Luna Park was one of them, and its brown bear, Samir, also needed help.

Four times the volunteers tried to rescue Samir from his filthy cage at the park, which is an hour from the Baghdad Zoo. But the first two attempts were unsuccessful because of equipment errors: the sedative dart gun didn't work and the transport cage was too small. On the third attempt, a more astonishing barrier stood in their way.

"We darted the bear," said Whittington-Jones, "but he didn't react at all. We darted him again, and he kept wandering around his cage. Another dart was administered. He staggered a bit but all in all appeared quite unfazed."

The rescue team was baffled. Why was Samir so resistant to the drugs? A Luna Park staffer finally solved the mystery. "The keepers used to drink alcohol in the evenings," Whittington-Jones said, "and the bear drank right along with them. We were dealing with an alcohol-addicted bear."

Would a fourth dart kill Samir? There was no way of knowing. But the volunteers decided to take that chance. "He appeared to be going down," Whittington-Jones recalled. "But after fifteen minutes, we had to admit defeat and go home."

On the last rescue attempt, a new strategy came into play. The door to Samir's enclosure was removed, a transport cage was pushed against the opening, and a serving of burned rice was used to draw him in.

"The cage was winched into the sky and plonked on the back of the truck," Whittington-Jones said. "Along the highway, over the bridge, into the Green Zone, and past the palace with a bear on the back of the truck must have been quite a sight."

Lifting "Last Man Standing" over the zoo wall and onto a waiting Army transport truck. We drove him across town to the Baghdad Zoo in the middle of a large convoy while people stared and waved.

FOUR

BLACK MARKET HORSES

Captain Sumner questioning local Iraqis during the recovery of Saddam's Arabian horses. Sixteen horses were located and brought to the Baghdad Zoo, where they are thriving.

"EVERY MAN WHO LOVES A HORSE is as good a man as he who is generous to the poor." Muhammad, the Prophet of Islam, is thought to have said that almost fourteen hundred years ago. The horse he was describing was the proud and graceful Arabian, native to the ancient Middle East, bred for loyalty, intelligence, beauty, and endurance.

Iraqi dictator Saddam Hussein cherished the Arabian horses he stabled at a palace not far from the Baghdad Zoo. But like the zoo animals, the horses vanished when the bombs began to fall.

Many believe President Hussein smuggled the horses out of Baghdad when he fled U.S. forces. After all, he was known for gathering the best Arabians money could buy, horses worth millions. But once Hussein went into hiding, their fate was anything but secure. Iraqi citizens believed the horses had fallen into the hands of dangerous black market traders, to be sold to the highest bidder.

Dr. Abu Bakker, an Iraqi veterinarian who cared for the horses before the war, did not believe that dire prediction. He was sure many of the animals were still living near Baghdad and pleaded with Captain Sumner and the zoo volunteers for help with recovering them.

Was it possible? So many animals had been butchered for food. Could the mares and stallions have been spared? Dr. Farah Murrani and Brendan Whittington-Jones met with Dr. Bakker to try to find out.

They pored though stacks of documents proving the herd had indeed been worth millions. The purest Arabian bloodlines on earth, they were possibly descendants of the horses the historic warrior Saladin rode into battle against the European Crusaders in the middle of the twelfth century. Dr. Murrani and Whittington-Jones agreed to present Dr. Bakker's request to the rest of the rescue team.

Captain Sumner, Lawrence Anthony, and representatives from the U.S. government agreed with Dr. Murrani and Whittington-Jones. The horses were too precious to be abandoned. Days later the search was on.

One fact that improved the odds was Dr. Murrani's remarkable gift of language. She speaks English and many dialects of Arabic fluently. Even her accents are flawless, making it possible for her to go undercover and pose as a person from virtually any Middle Eastern nation in order to collect information about the horses.

After questioning dangerous people in dangerous places, Dr. Murrani discovered what Dr. Bakker had suspected all along. Some of the horses—forty-six, the rumors claimed—had been stashed at a racetrack and stable near Abu Ghraib prison.

"Some people called that area RPG [rocket-propelled grenade] alley," Captain Sumner said. "It was a bad, bad place." Careful

Race day at the horse track west of Baghdad. Less than a month after the invasion, the track was back in operation, racing horses twice a week. Forty-six stolen Arabian horses were known to have been taken to the track and hidden in the warren of stables. Only sixteen were recovered.

ARABIAN HORSE FAST FACTS

Saddam Hussein loved Arabian horses and even put them on some of his country's currency. He was not alone in his affection. Arabians have been honored in Iraq for centuries. They carried ancient travelers across the savage heat of the desert. They even took the Prophet Muhammad into heaven, according to the Islamic faith.

These fast facts will tell you a little more about the Arabian horse breed, vastly popular in the Middle East and all over the world.

Scientific name: *Equus caballus*

Adult size: 14.1 to 15.1 hands (57 inches to 61 inches from hoof to shoulder)

Adult weight: 800 to 1,100 pounds

Coloration: Bay (brown coat/black mane), gray (gray coat and mane), chestnut (reddish brown coat and mane), black (black coat and mane), and roan (any of the other colors blended with white hairs, causing a lightening effect)

Normal diet: Herbivorous—hay (often alfalfa in the United States) and grain mixtures

Little-known facts: Arabian horses have stronger, denser bones than other horse breeds. One ancient Bedouin legend says Allah (God) created the Arabian by combining the four winds. The horses were endowed with special qualities—swiftness from the east wind, mental excellence from the west, a keen spirit from the north, and physical endurance from the south.

Horses in downtown Baghdad. Although donkeys were more common, it was not unusual to see horses pulling carts of food, electronics, or other goods throughout the city.

planning would be essential, or the rescue mission would fail and the consequences could be fatal.

Dr. Bakker discovered several of the grooms responsible for keeping the Arabians shiny and sleek had been employed as jockeys by the racetrack owners. Together, they tried to map out the grounds to help lay the groundwork for the rescue mission. Dr. Murrani, Whittington-Jones, and Ali, their driver and protector, visited the track on race days to get a better idea of how much opposition they might come up against.

"There were huge crowds," Whittington-Jones said. Would the crowds give up the valuable animals peacefully? It was impossible to know for sure. But with military assistance, the team decided they had to try.

Three rescue attempts were made. The first was scrapped when military engineers suffered equipment failure. The second, a larger raid scheduled to include troops approved by high-ranking U.S. administrators overseeing the war, failed when the leadership decided it was too dangerous.

"They were chicken and bailed out on us the afternoon before we were scheduled to move," Whittington-Jones said.

Attempt three was their last chance. So Captain Sumner, Whittington-Jones, and Dr. Murrani decided to go with an all-volunteer team they could count on and whatever equipment they could cobble together.

On one of the hottest mornings of the year, 130 degrees, Captain Sumner turned to Marine Captain Gavino Rivas and said, "I'm going to go save some horses. Want to come along?" Captain Rivas flashed what Captain Sumner called a "rock star grin." He and his buddies were on board.

With one Bradley tank, a couple of rickety Iraqi cattle transport trucks, three U.S. Army photographers, and a crew of ten or eleven determined volunteers, there would be no turning back. Confusion and resistance turned a two-hour mission into a six-hour brawl. When the dust cleared, the team discovered that only sixteen of the horses stabled were Hussein's Arabians. Where were the others? The possibilities were endless.

Thieves responsible for abducting the Arabians were arrested and taken into military custody, as the horses were loaded onto the transport vehicles. "One horse stepped on a rusted area of the truck, and its hoof went right through the floor," Whittington-Jones said. "It was chaos. Blood was gushing down his leg, and the rope around the horse's neck was now dangerously tight."

Captain Sumner worked to cut the rope as one of Dr. Bakker's grooms scrambled under the truck to push the horse's leg back up through the split in the floor—but not before he pulled a shard of metal out of the wound. Dr. Bakker worried the horse would be lame, unable to walk. He worried it would have to be put down. But after medical attention, the Arabian eventually healed.

TOP: A recovered Arabian is loaded onto a truck for transport.

BOTTOM: The rescued Arabians went first to the University of Baghdad, then to the Baghdad Zoo. Despite the mission's breaking almost all the "proper" rules for transporting animals, everyone arrived safely at their destination.

One of the Arabians at the track was recovering from an injury to his head.

The Arabians being exercised under the watchful eyes of the 1st Cavalry Division.

NEW STABLE UNVEILED

Iraqi citizens witnessed the opening of a new indoor horse stable, adjacent to the Baghdad Zoo, in December 2007. The management of the stable is currently a part of the U.S. Army's 15th Brigade Support Battalion, 2nd Brigade Combat Team, 1st Cavalry Division's duties. With twenty stalls, an arena, and a birthing area, it provides the prized Arabians with a safe headquarters where ordinary people can watch the horses exercise and train.

The horses were moved to the University of Baghdad stable, where International Fund for Animal Welfare (IFAW) staff member Mariette Hopley temporarily managed their recovery. "She was a powerhouse," Captain Sumner recalled. "She really knew how to get things done." Donations from the U.S. Army, the city of Baghdad, and private groups made building a new stable adjacent to the Baghdad Zoo possible. U.S. Army Cavalry troops like Staff Sergeant Robert Bussell cared for the valuable Arabians once they were installed in their new home. Personnel from the 1st Cavalry Division—famous for their equestrian skills—worked with dedicated Iraqis like veterinarian Dr. Wasseem Wali, to train the staff on how to care properly for the recovered animals. Their high standard of training and dedication set an example for the zoo staff that continues to this day.

They were purebred Arabians with bloodlines that went back hundreds, if not thousands, of years. We had DNA tests and records to prove it. These were the top of the top Arabians. Their spirits, their abilities were incredible.

We were able to identify these horses and went through what turned out to be a traumatic event for all of us. We moved in, and it was an extremely long, tedious day and a lot more dangerous than we had

anticipated. We didn't regret it because the horses were so important.

Relationships were built on the common desire to help the horses. We spent a lot of time talking about the politics, the war, us versus them, Muslims, Christians. . . . But it doesn't matter: your background, your politics, nothing. The only thing that mattered was making sure the animals were okay. It makes me think: if we could put all that aside for the animals, what else could we do?

Captain Sumner and Captain Gavino Rivas, U.S. Marines Civil Affairs Officer, at the University of Baghdad stables following the recovery operation. During their time in Iraq, Captain Rivas and his squad of Marines became experts in locating stolen historical artifacts and transporting horses.

29

FIVE

PELICAN BRIEF

Entry sign to the Luna Park zoo. Notice the Dalmatian in the lower left corner of the sign. Dogs were one of the main attractions of the zoo, along with bears, lions, and pigs.

THANKS TO HIS REPUTATION AS "THE zoo man," Captain Sumner received dozens, even hundreds of animal rescue tips from troops and citizens all over Baghdad. One tip sent him to Luna Park, a privately owned petting zoo about an hour's drive from the Baghdad Zoo. He found the animals were in "a miserable state."

"A pelican, sometimes called Buddy, had been tethered to a pole with a three-foot rope. He couldn't move. He had no water, which is real bad for a waterbird," Captain Sumner said. The picture he took to document the abuse sparked the rescue team to action. "It was key to closing that place down."

With support from the U.S. Army, Captain Sumner's volunteer crew, and several rescue organizations, including Care for the Wild International, the Thula Thula Game Reserve, and IFAW, the

One of the pelicans at Luna Park. The bird did not have access to clean water, food, or shade, and was tethered to a short length of rope. When U.S. officials asked why we closed down the zoo, all we had to do was show them this picture.

International Fund for Animal Welfare, the animals of Luna Park, including the stranded pelican, were gathered and carried back to the Baghdad Zoo for medical attention and long-term care.

Giant seabirds like pelicans aren't what you expect to see in a desert war zone. So creating a habitat took a little creative thinking.

Pelicans in their temporary enclosure.

PELICAN FAST FACTS

Pelicans look awkward on land, but they have lived and thrived on earth for millions of years because they are skilled swimmers, hunters, and fliers. They are social birds that generally tolerate other pelicans and some other breeds of birds as well. Dalmatian pelicans sometimes fly and hunt with cormorants. Once the companion birds spot and dive for fish, the pelicans drop to the water and use their pouched beaks to grab and "net" their catch. Their appetites are so enormous, some fishermen believe they can impact the catch needed for human consumption.

Scientific name: *Pelecanus crispus*

Adult size: 4 to 6 feet (body only), 6- to 11-foot wingspan

Adult weight: 10 to 17 pounds

Coloration: Variations of white and light brown feathers

Normal diet: Carnivorous—4 pounds of saltwater fish a day normally, but pelicans will eat other things like reptiles or smaller birds if necessary

Little-known facts: A group of pelicans is known as a pod. Seagulls sometimes sit on the heads of pelicans to sneak bites of food. And fossilized pelicans date back as far as forty million years.

"Mariette Hopley built the pelican a huge temporary pool made of a tarp and sandbags," Captain Sumner said. "He was so happy. His recovery was almost immediate." Once the Iraqis realized a pelican was on display at the zoo, a strange thing happened.

"Animals started coming out of the woodwork," Captain Sumner recalled. "Before we knew it, people were lining up to return animals."

Not all of the pelicans got along, according to Dr. Murrani. "Another pelican we rescued got some bad lacerations on its beak and pouch—in a fight," she recalled. "We stitched it up, but the beak started to die."

According to experts at the U.S. Department of Energy's science

After the pelicans were moved, Brendan Whittington-Jones transformed this building into a large aviary.

education office, the base of a bird's beak is bone, attached to the animal's skull. But the part that protrudes beyond that bone is a calcium compound called keratin. Fingernails are also made of keratin.

Losing part of the beak wasn't necessarily life threatening for the pelican, soon to be named Bell. But not being able to eat certainly would be. "So we fed him by hand for a while," Dr. Murrani said.

The same sassy attitude that resulted in the wounds helped the disabled pelican survive. "He wound up fighting for food," she said. "He was actually faster than the other pelicans when it came to catching the fish. He was really fun."

We found this pelican tethered in the middle of a nearly dry pool, with about three feet of rope wrapped around its leg. He couldn't go anywhere. He was stuck. Since these birds are waterbirds, they obviously needed water. This one was dull gray, he hadn't been taken care of, there was a dead swan in the same enclosure. It was a bad experience.

I took a picture of him when we first got there, and it was my picture of this pelican sitting in the middle of this dismal, muck-filled place that triggered a lot of the rest of the events.

Later on Mariette Hopley from the International Fund for Animal Welfare helped us build a pelican pond: a bunch of sandbags and tarp, plus a couple of hoses so we could drain out the muck. It was one of these impromptu things—we worked as quickly as possible to make the animals more comfortable.

Almost immediately, the pelican hit that water, and he stayed there. That was his new place, and he claimed it. Within days you could see the change. His feathers were back to their original color, and he cleaned himself up; it was amazing to see the transformation of this pelican.

Eventually we acquired another pelican, brought in by an Iraqi. After that, we rebuilt another enclosure to give the pelicans a lot more space to play in. We added some other waterfowl. That first pelican was the trigger for shutting down Luna Park, but everyone else did so much—built the pond, the enclosure, donated other pelicans—another example where everyone chipped in to make something happen.

I'll always keep that picture of the pelican with me. It was a tipping point. It was an amazing time.

SIX

LOVABLE LUMPY

Lumpy at his new home in the Baghdad Zoo, after his hair began to grow back from his full shave.

DROMEDARIES, ONE-HUMPED CAMELS, are known for their ability to survive the extremes of the Arabian landscape. They do not store water in their humps. Fat is actually stored there—extra calories to burn. But when camels perspire to reduce their body temperature, the thick fur that covers their sweaty skin keeps the moisture from evaporating too quickly, so they stay hydrated. And their oval-shaped blood cells—most mammal blood cells are circular—can squeeze through their vessels even when water is scarce and they are dehydrated.

Captain Sumner's favorite rescue animal was a dromedary named Lumpy. The water storage and special hydration skills nature gave him kept him alive—but just barely—until help could arrive. War nearly cost him his life.

An ex-Iraqi Republican Guard soldier works with U.S. troops to move Lumpy into the Humvee; next stop, the Baghdad Zoo.

Housed in Luna Park, Lumpy's time was running out. His keepers had abandoned him. But he wasn't well cared for to begin with. On top of starvation and dehydration, his fur was severely matted, and his skin was riddled with mange.

What is mange? It is an infestation of microscopic mites, tiny insects that bite and burrow and cause inflammation, severe itching, and some hair loss. "Lumpy had a bad case of it," Captain Sumner said. "He was a very neglected young camel."

Without immediate medical care, Lumpy might not make it. That's where Captain Sumner's U.S. Army Humvee came in handy. Humvees weren't meant for animal transport, but Lumpy needed to get to the Baghdad Zoo, and pronto. So a Humvee would have to do.

Iraqi citizens stepped in to help Captain Sumner and other volunteers lead the wobbly camel from his holding pen to concrete stairs near a Luna Park exit. Backed up against the staircase was the military vehicle. Getting Lumpy down the stairs and onto the Humvee was quite a challenge.

"It was almost laughable," Captain Sumner remembered. Some of the volunteers were pulling the camel's lead. Others stood behind him, pushing his flanks. But Lumpy was resistant.

BELOW: Iraqis helping to load Lumpy onto the back of the Humvee at Luna Park.

RIGHT: Captain Sumner, Lawrence Anthony (right), and zoo staffers ride with Lumpy to the zoo.

Cargo straps kept Lumpy from standing up as the Humvee rolled across town.

"He wasn't sure it was a good idea," Captain Sumner said. "But eventually we got him loaded," along with baby pigs, goats, dogs, monkeys, the pelican, and a few other smaller animals—some on board with Lumpy, the rest in one of the other three Humvees. Several of the volunteers, including Captain Sumner, rode with Lumpy to keep him calm as they made their way across town.

An enemy sniper was spotted in the area. "We were in a tunnel, and we stopped until the area was cleared and it was safe to go on," Captain Sumner said. "We moved out fairly quickly, and all made it back to the zoo alive."

At the Baghdad Zoo Lumpy's medical care could begin.

"His fur was so filthy, like plates of concrete, we decided to shave

Dromedaries, also known as Arabian camels, have been a part of the Middle Eastern landscape since prehistoric times. Some historians believe they were domesticated as pack animals and desert transportation in about 4000 B.C. Others disagree and say it was more likely 1400 B.C. But because they can travel so far without drinking water, the sturdy animals have been crucial to Middle Eastern culture and survival for most of recorded human history.

Scientific name: *Camelus dromedarius*

Adult size: 7 feet tall at the hump

Adult weight: Up to 1,600 pounds

Coloration: Various shades of light to dark tan

Normal diet: Herbivorous—virtually any vegetation it can forage in the desert

Little-known facts: Two rows of thick eyelashes protect the dromedary's eyes from sudden dust storms. The camels can go more than ten days without drinking water, but once they break the dry spell, they can guzzle thirty gallons in under fifteen minutes. The llama, alpaca, guanaco, and vicuña are the camel's South American cousins.

When we finally got Lumpy out of his cage, he found a patch of grass and he started rolling and rolling and would not stop. It was either the first time he'd seen grass or the first time he was able to lie out on it completely.

Imagine driving across Baghdad, people shooting at you, a lot of traffic, all the sounds and signs of war around you, and a camel's head resting on your shoulder. It was almost too weird to believe.

Once we got to the zoo, it took almost as much effort to get him off the truck as it did to get him on it. But finally we twisted his tail, and he hopped right off. After that, we had to evaluate him medically. We literally had to shave him bald. Whittington-Jones had Lumpy's head in his lap while Dr. Jose Lozada, a veterinarian with the 490th Civil Affairs Battalion, shaved him down. Everyone invested a lot of time and effort in Lumpy. He grew up with us at the zoo.

Brendan Whittington-Jones, left, and Dr. Jose Lozada, shaving off the last of a sedated Lumpy's matted fur in order to check for mange and provide medical treatment.

poor Lumpy," Captain Sumner said. Lumpy's recovery began almost immediately. Medicine cleared up the mange infestation, and a steady diet helped him regain his strength. "He's still there at the zoo," Captain Sumner said. "He's twice the size he was. And they brought in a female camel in 2007—put him in a large enclosure with his new mate. Guess you could say Lumpy lived happily ever after. One day there might even be little camels!"

Lumpy's fur was matted with dried mud, feces, and tangled hair. The fur was like a shell of armor and it had to be hand-trimmed, piece by piece.

SEVEN
LIONHEARTED

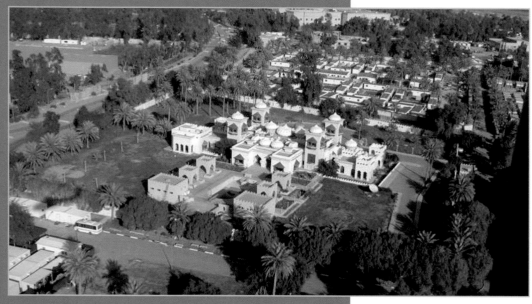

One of many smaller palaces located near the main Republican Palace.

As AN ADULT SON OF THE DICTATOR SADDAM HUSSEIN, Uday Hussein was once set to inherit his father's kingdom, but his explosive anger cost him that legacy.

Keeping big cats—lions and cheetahs—was one of Uday Hussein's hobbies, until the bombs fell and he was forced to run and hide. He abandoned his 258-room palace and his other living quarters, along with the animals he kept there. He left the cats locked in their enclosures to die of starvation and dehydration. U.S. troops from the army's 3rd Infantry Division discovered one collection as they explored one of his domains.

After moving room to room, stepping over bodies and rubble, Staff Sergeant Darren Swain and his fellow soldiers came to an adjacent concrete compound by the Tigris River. As Sergeant Swain pushed the door open, he thought his eyes were deceiving him, according to an article in the *Chicago Tribune*. He "saw a big old tail go past," he said—a lion's tail, the first of three, one male, two female. He later found two cheetahs and a small group of ostriches, along with sheep (food for the big cats) in other enclosures—all hovering near death.

Some of Uday's big cats had puzzling companions: dogs. The adult lions, carnivores at the top of the food chain, were starving to death. The dogs were starving by their sides, no bars or fences between them. And yet the lions had not eaten the dogs. Why? According to animal experts, the lions had probably bonded with the dogs as cubs.

In another abandoned palace, two female lions were soon nicknamed Xena and Heather. The male was called Brutus. As the fighting raged on, Xena gave birth to a litter of six healthy cubs. She was a good mother, and together with Heather, kept her litter safe. Brutus, unlike most male lions, doted on the babies, according to Captain Sumner. "He would actually play with the cubs and let them crawl all over him," he said.

In war, infantry soldiers like Sergeant Swain have other duties to fulfill, so the team from the Baghdad Zoo was asked to step in, to care for Uday's animals and guide them back to health. Lawrence Anthony, Brendan Whittington-Jones, Dr. Farah Murrani, Dr. Barbara Maas, and WildAid expert Stephan Bognar were all eager to answer the call.

According to a report in *The Oakland Tribune*, Bognar, who arrived from his animal rescue work in Cambodia, flew from Jordan to Iraq with only a single change of clothes and no idea what he might find when he arrived. Dr. Murrani and Whittington-Jones went on frequent food runs. Each time they had to pass armed guards charged with keeping suspicious vehicles out of the Green Zone, the safest part of Baghdad, where Uday's palace was located.

"It was hard some days," Dr. Murrani recalled, "going through the checkpoint with a trunkful of meat to feed the lions. At first, they

TOP: Two of Xena's cubs at one of the smaller palace zoos.

ABOVE: The Lion Dog of Baghdad. When the cubs were integrated with the rest of the lion population at the zoo, the dog would sit outside of the cage for days waiting to see his friends. It was too dangerous to let them stay together because of the other lions, which had not grown up with him.

In most cultures, on most continents, the lion has been legendary for centuries, in fact and in fiction. Is it any wonder world leaders, good and bad, have adopted the lion as their personal totems? Symbols of royalty and power, lions are at the top of the food chain with no natural enemies. (Correction: They have no natural enemies, other than man.)

Scientific name: *Panthera leo*

Adult size: 4 feet 7 inches to 8 feet 2 inches long

Adult weight: Up to 550 pounds

Coloration: Light tan with brown points

Normal diet: Carnivorous—impala, zebra, wildebeest, wild boar

Little-known facts: Lions are social animals, communicating with sounds, touch, and even facial expressions. Only one big cat is larger than the lion, and that's the tiger. Lion images have been part of human history for as long as thirty-two thousand years, as rock art, cave paintings, and even artifacts carved from ivory and stone. As with all big cats, the lion population is on the decline.

RIGHT: Brutus, the large male lion, at one of the smaller palace zoos. Brutus was kept in this smaller enclosure during feeding times so that the rest of the animals would have a chance to eat.

FAR RIGHT: One of the lion cubs at the Baghdad Zoo. The cubs were very playful and enjoyed interacting with visitors.

were like, 'Yeah, right.' But then they got to know us and it was a hoot. They called me Lion Lady."

Whittington-Jones lived in a hotel within the Green Zone. On ordinary days, he went through the checkpoint to the zoo in the morning and checked on the pride of lions on his way back home. But when a sick lioness made him break his routine, it may have saved his life.

"As I arrived at the enclosure and was unlocking the doors, a huge car bomb went off," he remembered. "Even the lions ran outside into the open area in surprise, and they usually didn't react to the sound of small-arms fire or helicopters flying past their enclosures. The interim president of Iraq was killed in that blast, along with eleven other people. Was it a coincidence or something else, the fact that I didn't go through the checkpoint? Who knows? But it was spooky."

Fortunately, most meat runs didn't put the zoo team in that kind of danger, but when butchered meat wasn't available, some life-and-death choices had to be made. For four dollars, the lions could feast on an

Two controversies clouded the rescue of the lions of Baghdad. Four lions escaped the Baghdad Zoo during the early shock and awe bombing raids. Panicked and frightened, two of the lions attacked soldiers patrolling the streets of Baghdad and had to be put down. It was a tragic day for everyone involved.

The second controversy was not so easy to understand. As Captain Sumner and his team began to bring the animals back to good health, one international rescue group decided Uday's lions deserved better than a lifetime behind bars. They longed to see the pride returned to Africa and released into the wild.

On the surface, it may have seemed like a good idea. But the adult lions moved from Uday Hussein's palace to the zoo—Xena and Heather—had been declawed. Without these important tools, the lions would be helpless in the wild. And while the international volunteers were kind and generous, sharing their time and expertise to help the four-legged war zone survivors, in the end, the lions belonged to the people of Iraq.

When Iraqi zookeepers and city officials stood firm on their decision to keep the lions in Baghdad rather than send them to an African sanctuary, some volunteers were offended. But Captain Sumner, Whittington-Jones, and Dr. Murrani knew the difference between helping and taking full control. Once the Iraqi people stepped up to care for their exotic zoo animals, it was crucial for the outsiders to step down gracefully.

animal very common in Baghdad, a donkey from the street market. It was never an easy choice, but at times it was the only way to keep the lions alive.

No wonder caring for new life—the six lion cubs—was one of Dr. Murrani's favorite duties. With the cubs, the struggles of the war seemed a little bit farther away. "They were so cute and little," she said, "but still had lion instincts. And they all had beautiful eyes. When they looked at you, they really *looked* at you."

Whittington-Jones, who had observed lions in his native South Africa, agreed. "The pride of lions at the palace became a bit of a soft point for me," he said. "I always looked forward to spending time at their enclosure. It's not often on a game reserve that you get so close to lions, and they certainly don't have an affinity for humans. The lions at the palace were by no means tame, but they did enjoy lying against the fence near us as we chatted on the other side."

That ease with humans sometimes put the lions in additional danger. They faced bombs and starvation because of the war. They faced potentially toxic waste at the hands of careless people.

"A major issue was people throwing litter into the area, either for fun, to tease the animals, or because they thought the animals were hungry. It was annoying and a real risk to the animals," Whittington-Jones said. "If an animal ingested a piece of plastic or something similar, it could be deadly."

Moving the palace lions to the zoo wouldn't solve all the problems, but it would give the animals a bigger enclosure and steady supervision. So Whittington-Jones and the vets joined with a team from the U.S. Army to make it happen. Like the bear from Luna Park, the lions were darted so they would sleep in transit. Unlike the bear from Luna Park, the lions responded normally to the sedative and were loaded onto canvas stretchers and transported as a family to their new home at the zoo.

The lions are a symbol of Iraq, and I remember one guy who wanted to breed them and open a lion park. They were very large lions with large teeth that needed to be treated very carefully. One of the more unusual things that happened was one day one of the zoo workers had another animal get into the lion enclosure by accident.

He was an older guy, who every day when we saw him would say, "Hello, I'm Salman. I've been with the zoo for thirty-five years." It was the only English he knew, and every time we saw him, he'd say that. Anyway, without even thinking, Salman took a large stick and ran into the center of the lion enclosure. There were about eight full-sized lions surrounding him, but he just walked in and took care of the situation. It was

amazing. I can't believe he wasn't eaten.

We played with some of the cubs from the time they were born. While they were young, we could play with them without fear of being torn up. They did have claws, but they were like little kittens. Several zoo workers adopted these cubs and took personal pride in them, as if they were members of their own families.

The bonds among the animals, the soldiers and volunteers, and the zoo workers were a good thing to build upon. Because we went there, we invaded Iraq, and here we were months later working with several of these guys who had been in the Iraqi Army. We watched them gain pride in what they were doing. Without these small moments, I don't know if we would have been as successful at the zoo.

One of the cubs as an adult. Although we did play with the cubs when they were little, we stopped when it became too dangerous.

EIGHT

CHEETAH TIME

ABOVE: Specialist Erin McLoughlin visiting with Lucky and Chance during one of our weekly medical check-ups.

RIGHT: Lucky resting in his temporary enclosure. Both of our cheetahs were moved to a large, open air habitat in early 2004 in order to keep them happy and healthy.

IRAQI DICTATOR SADDAM HUSSEIN RAN his nation with an iron fist, using power to collect wealth as his people struggled to survive. His adult son Uday enjoyed a playboy lifestyle, thanks to his father's regime. Caged within the palace grounds, in addition to Uday's lions, were two cheetahs sometimes called Lucky and Chance.

Such hopeful names were adopted by rescue workers, but not by the U.S. Army and certainly not by the man who abandoned them. Left to die without water or food, these exotic pets were unlucky by any compassionate measures.

Once Lucky and Chance were moved from the palace to their supervised enclosures, their friendly nature captured Captain Sumner's imagination. "They had been declawed," he said, "and they were pretty tame, never gave us much trouble." They were also admired

Staggering speeds of up to 70 miles per hour make the cheetah the fastest land mammal on earth. But as swift as it may be, it has not been able to escape the threat of extinction. Rare to begin with—50 to 75 percent of all cheetah cubs are lost before adulthood—the shrinking habitat and food sources have dropped the total population to dangerous lows. Fewer than 13,000 individuals survive on the African continent.

Scientific name: *Acinonyx jubatus*

Adult size: 53 inches long

Adult weight: Up to 140 pounds

Coloration: Golden brown with black or dark brown spots

Normal diet: Carnivorous—small antelopes, in the wild

Little-known facts: Cheetahs were once trained to hunt with human masters. The legendary emperor Akbar the Great of East India, who is said to have taken the throne at age thirteen in 1556, once kept as many as a thousand cheetahs in his palace stable. Cheetahs can purr, chirp, and growl as they exhale breath, but they cannot roar. The cheetah's closest living relative is the cougar.

Taking a time-out from a medical check-up to play with a new toy.

for their sleek beauty by visitors who came to the zoo.

Captain Sumner hatched a plan he called "cheetah time." As troops, officers, and dignitaries toured the Baghdad Zoo—as they saw how important the work was, how it was building a bridge between the U.S. military and the Iraqi people—Captain Sumner explained the challenges of keeping the animals fed and healthy. He gained a stream of support, and those supporters were rewarded with "cheetah time."

Dozens of photographs of generous zoo supporters and the big spotted cats turned up in scrapbooks and on websites around the world.

Captain Sumner wasn't the only one focused on cheetah play. Experts from IFAW offered the pair enrichment tricks, to keep their minds and bodies healthy. Sandbags filled with hay, then soaked in excrement and animal blood were tossed into the cheetahs' cage. According to IFAW journals, the siblings found the smelly toys fascinating and loved swatting them around like house cats with catnip.

From time to time, Chance battles the chronic pain of arthritis in her left hind ankle. But on the whole, both the cheetahs have adjusted well to life in the Baghdad Zoo.

The cheetahs had been stuck in an enclosure with several lions and the "lion dog." But we found out later they were Uday's personal cheetahs. He used to put big, expensive collars on these cheetahs, put them in his car, drive them around to restaurants, and hang out with them. They were, essentially, large domestic cats.

Obviously, they were wild animals, and we were always leery about that. However, they were declawed and they were very friendly. You could walk in with the cheetahs and play with them; they would flip over, let you rub their stomachs. Everyone just loved these animals.

When you go to the zoos in the United States, you see cheetahs behind bars, or you see them on television chasing things down. But you never see them as "pettable." I'll always remember walking around the Baghdad Zoo with a couple of cheetahs trailing behind me.

Captain Sumner and Specialist McLoughlin giving Chance a weekly medical check-up. As a veterinary technician, Specialist McLoughlin provided a significant amount of the routine on-site medical care for the animal population.

NINE

TIGER TRAGEDY AND TRIUMPH

Order:– Carnivora

الرتبة ـ آكلة اللحوم

Family:– Felidae

العائلة ـ السنورية

Spp :– Tiger

الأسم الشائع ـ بيراسبوي

Origin:– India

الموطن ـ الهند

ملاحظة ـ برجى عدم التحرش بالحيوان أو اطعامه

ABOVE: Sign outside of the tiger enclosure. Each exhibit had a sign like this to educate visitors about the animals.

RIGHT: Mandor resting inside his enclosure.

IN ASIA, IT IS THE TIGER, NOT THE LION, that claims the title King of Beasts. An animal known for its strength, agility, and striking striped coloration, it has been adopted as an icon by football teams, gas stations, and cereal boxes, not to mention as a year within the Chinese zodiac. That power and near-universal appeal are part of what made Malooh so important to the Baghdad Zoo and the zoo volunteers desperate to save him.

Once dazed and sluggish from starvation and water deprivation, the rare Bengal tiger fought his way back to majestic stature. A showcase animal for the zoo and the recovery effort, Malooh was often admired by important visitors from a bench securely installed a safe distance from the bars of his cage. Most understood his danger and his beauty.

But calm can be mistaken for tameness. And beauty may have

How did two American-born tigers wind up seven thousand miles from home? According to the U.S. Army's DefenseLink news, they were a gift, "a goodwill gesture from The Conservators' Center in North Carolina, a breeding sanctuary for endangered species."

Summers will be hotter in Hope's and Riley's new home than it was in North Carolina—about twenty to thirty degrees hotter, according to their respective average summer temperatures. But as the new stars of the Baghdad Zoo, they'll have all the pool time and all the admiration they can handle to help even the score.

How much does it cost to fly a pair of two-year-old tigers halfway around the world? The answer is a whopping $66,000, according to the Department of Defense. But the U. S. Embassy was kind enough to pick up the tab.

Not everyone was in favor of the gift. Actress Kim Basinger and animal rights organization People for the Ethical Treatment of Animals (PETA) protested, citing the destruction and loss of life in the zoo after the war began in March 2003. But five years of hard work have carried the war-torn zoo into the future with many improvements and the promise of even more.

Iraq is a lot hotter than North Carolina, but Riley's splash pool helped the young tiger adapt.

tempted one wayward soldier to climb over the railing, crawl through an access panel, push through the hedge, and slip his arm into the tiger's cage. Regardless of reasoning, the end result proved tragic in September 2003 for one soldier and one beast.

Panic hit when Malooh's teeth sank into the soldier's arm. A bullet from a fellow soldier's gun left its chamber. Malooh died from internal bleeding.

Blood, sweat, and tears invested in bringing Malooh back to good health had been wasted. Trust painstakingly built between Iraqi staffers and the U.S. Army through hard work and shared determination had been shattered. Without question, the tiger's death was senseless and shameful.

"The soldiers don't have the right to behave like that," said zoo director Dr. Adel Salman Mousa. "That was the most precious and valuable animal in the whole zoo. It was fourteen years old and had been born here."

Captain Sumner was also heartbroken. "It was terrible," he said, "one of the worst days of my life."

As he, Brendan Whittington-Jones, Dr. Murrani, and Wasseem Wali did the autopsy, they confirmed what they already knew. As they gathered evidence—followed the blood trail from the cage back to the bench—every mistake the soldier had made was crystal clear. The facts didn't bring Malooh back, but they did begin to repair the damage.

The first soldier was wrong to get so close to the unpredictable tiger, and he paid with his life for his bad judgment. But the second soldier didn't shoot the tiger for sport or to be unkind. He shot in response to his fear. He shot to save his impulsive friend. The Iraqi zookeepers couldn't help expressing their grief. But they accepted that Malooh's death was no more than a horrifying mistake.

Mandor, the second tiger rescued by the zoo team, was the only tiger now. The cat still swam in his pool at the zoo. He still carried his

TIGER FAST FACTS

Loners at heart, tigers are the largest big cats on earth. They once reigned over Asia and India, but today, they are endangered, their numbers dwindling. Fewer than fifteen hundred Bengal tigers still exist in the wild. Roughly five hundred Siberian tigers exist in the wild. But captive breeding programs have been very successful.

Scientific name: *Panthera tigris*

Adult size: Up to 13 feet long

Adult weight: Up to 600 pounds

Coloration: Gold and tan with black stripes

Normal diet: Carnivorous—virtually any small or medium-size animals in their territory

Little-known facts: Most tigers have a hundred stripes or more, and the pattern is unique to each tiger, the way fingerprints are to humans. The patterns would remain on the tiger skin even if you shaved the fur away.

One of the zoo's newest residents explores his new home.

orange traffic cone in and out of the water. He still played with his smelly sandbag toys. But something was missing. Something wasn't right.

"I promised to make it up to them," Captain Sumner said. And slowly, trust was restored. Redemption finally came in August 2008, several years after Captain Sumner had returned home, with two new tigers from North Carolina named Riley and Hope.

We had two tigers, and they were pretty neat. One of the civil affairs officers who helped us used to make a joke. She said they reminded her of tiger soup. The two tigers had these small enclosures, with a six-by-six-foot pool in each one. The pools weren't very large for big tigers. But she would always see their heads sticking out of the pool, with the rest of them submerged.

They were good animals. We didn't interact with them too much because they were tigers and they were wild. We had the one incident where one was shot, and that was tragic.

The army was interested in supplying new tigers to the zoo, and for a long time we tried to discourage that because the enclosures weren't up to par. But they rebuilt several enclosures, and two tiger cubs were shipped over from the states. Riley and Hope are doing very well, and it's an example of how the zoo is rebuilding itself, of how the Iraqis have stayed committed to it. I'm sure the tigers are going to be a good attraction for the families that have started to come visit the park.

Hope and Riley

TEN

BACK TO THE FUTURE

The Baghdad Zoo prior to its reopening. The large map on the right allowed visitors to locate animals and see all of the attractions at the zoo.

Several years have passed since Captain Sumner and his team of experts—Dr. Farah Murrani, Brendan Whittington-Jones, Lawrence Anthony, Specialist Erin McLoughlin, Wasseem Wali, and others—took action to save the abandoned animals at the Baghdad Zoo and beyond. They survived the dangers of war and moved on, though thousands of their fellow troops and citizens weren't as lucky.

Helping United States forces was dangerous for Iraqi citizens. People loyal to Saddam Hussein considered those Iraqis enemies. So Dr. Murrani was forced to leave her home. Death threats against her and her family members made it impossible to stay. For a time she toured the United States, speaking at zoos and learning from American veterinarians. She went on to South Africa, and now makes her home in the United Arab Emirates.

Brendan Whittington-Jones went to the United States to work in several local zoos, then went to help in the rebuilding of the Kabul Zoo in Afghanistan. After that he returned to South Africa for a time, then took a position with the Endangered Wildlife Trust's Wild Dog Advisory Group in Zululand. Explore his work at this website: www.ewt.org.za/species_wild_dogs.aspx.

Lawrence Anthony also went back to the Thula Thula Game Reserve and wrote his own book on the rescue of the Baghdad Zoo, *Babylon's Ark*, with coauthor Graham Spence. He founded the Earth Organization to help more animals in distress. His website is www.lawrenceanthony.co.za.

Erin McLoughlin traveled the world after her tour of duty ended, working with animal rescue organizations, expanding her veterinary knowledge, and sharing her stories of work at the Baghdad Zoo. She graduated from a Michigan university and plans to continue her work with animals.

As for Captain William Sumner, he finished his tour of duty, came home, and moved his family from Maryland to Nebraska, where he continues to serve his country and was promoted to major. He is also working on his doctorate in biodefense at George Mason University. He already has a master's in education and a master's in archaeology.

On July 19, 2003, the Baghdad Zoo, still heavily guarded by U.S. military personnel, reopened to the public. With a flurry of balloons and music, Iraqi citizens strolled back into the zoo they'd shared with their children before the country was invaded by coalition forces. The temperature rocketed to 112 degrees, and fewer than a hundred animals were on exhibit—a far cry from the zoo in its heyday. But the opening was a sign of hope, a glimpse of normal life.

According to a Reuters newspaper report on July 20, 2003, Emad

TOP: One of many signs announcing the opening of the Baghdad Zoo and Al Zawra park. Several of these signs were hung around the city since lack of electricity limited access to television and radio.

BOTTOM: Visitors to the zoo share stories with an American soldier. During the opening, children were able to interact directly with soldiers, exchange experiences, and learn about each other.

TOP: Dr. Barbara Maas examining two of Luna Park's porcupines. She was able to corral the animals using a garbage pail and load them into small kennels for their trip to the zoo.

BOTTOM: Several goats that were rescued from Luna Park. Since we did not have nearly enough cages, animals were loaded onto the Humvees wherever space could be found.

Abbas and his two-year-old son, Ali, were among the first returning visitors. "Ali wanted to see the animals," Abbas said in the article. "We haven't been able to enter this part for many months, but now it looks good."

Ali was as shy as Keena, the seven-month-old lion cub he studied through the safety of painted green bars. When the reporter asked if Ali was more afraid of Saddam Hussein or the lion, his father reportedly answered, "The lion; Saddam is gone now."

Other Baghdad residents agreed. "I feel safe here," said Ali Abdul Hussein, a taxi driver, to a reporter from the *Los Angeles Times*. "Before, we always felt someone was watching and listening to us. We didn't feel free."

Dr. Mousa, the zoo's director, said both visitors summed things up perfectly. Because all people and cars visiting the two-thousand-acre park are carefully searched by dozens of security workers, both U.S. and Iraqi, it has become a sanctuary. "This is the only place where Iraqis in Baghdad can breathe," he said in the same *Los Angeles Times* report.

Steady improvements have been made. An indoor equestrian stable and an exotic fish aquarium were opened; the tigers Hope and Riley arrived from North Carolina; even the amusement park and swimming pool were repaired and reopened, just beyond the zoo property.

The future is uncertain in many Iraqi communities. Battles are still being fought. But inside the giant gates of the Baghdad Zoo, hope endures.

"I would get frustrated, trying to keep the animals fed, scraping the money together to build enclosures, shutting down the black market dealers," Captain Sumner said. "All those things were hard, but the zoo actually helped me, personally.

RIGHT: Opening day at the Baghdad Zoo. On July 19, just months after the invasion of Iraq, the zoo was opened to the public.

Lawrence Anthony (left), Stephan Bognar (middle), and Captain Sumner (right), holding rescued dogs. All of these dogs were adopted and sent to the United States.

"Things were blowing up all around us," he continued. "We were fighting a war. But in this one place, at the zoo, we could fix something. We could do something good for the people we were trying to help. Right there in the middle of a war was this beautiful green park with grass and trees and lakes. It was an oasis in a shattered, concrete world."

Captain Sumner's favorite times were the early mornings, as the sun came up over Baghdad. "It was quiet," he said. "Well, relatively quiet. I could walk around and talk to each of the animals. 'How are you doing today?' I'd say. 'Is that leg healing up okay? Hey, this water isn't as bad as it was yesterday.' It didn't really matter what I said. It was just the sound of a soft, friendly voice that mattered. It was just me and the animals. And each one responded in its own way."

Not one of William Sumner's team members ever considered giving up on this mission. When it came to this rescue operation, and saving the Baghdad Zoo, the bottom line was pretty simple.

"We were a team, and we had a job to do—a tough one," Captain Sumner concluded. "But it was a time I'll never forget. It was an exercise in compassion, and that's something worth remembering."

LEFT: One of two tortoises at the zoo. He was found living under a broken water pipe, buried in mud.

BELOW: Zoo visitors watching lions inside of the enclosure's viewing area.

INTERVIEWS

Major William Sumner, interviews by Kelly Milner Halls, July 1, 2007; July 13, 2007; August 21, 2007; December 1, 2007; May 30, 2008; July 22, 2008; August 5, 2008; December 20, 2008.

Stephan Bognar, interviews by Kelly Milner Halls, June 5, 2008; June 13, 2008.

Louise Joubert (executive director, SanWild Wildlife Trust), interview by Kelly Milner Halls, June 12, 2008.

Yvette Taylor (public relations, SanWild Wildlife Trust), interview by Kelly Milner Halls, June 12, 2008.

Lawrence Anthony, interview by Kelly Milner Halls, June 16, 2008.

Brendan Whittington-Jones, interviews by Kelly Milner Halls, June 19, 2008; June 26, 2008; July 10, 2008; July 28, 2008; September 9, 2008.

Dr. Farah Murrani, interviews by Kelly Milner Halls, June 19, 2008; June 25, 2008; July 27, 2008.

Dr. Jackson Zee (International Fund for Animal Welfare veterinarian), interviews by Kelly Milner Halls, June 19, 2008; July 22, 2008.

Mariette Hopley, interview by Kelly Milner Halls, June 23, 2008.

Dr. Ellen Dierenfeld, interview by Kelly Milner Halls, August 8, 2008.

Dr. Martin R. Dinnes (director, product research and development, Natural Balance Zoological Formula), interview by Kelly Milner Halls, August 10, 2008.

Michlyn Hines (zoo operations supervisor, America's Teaching Zoo, Moorpark College, CA), interview by Kelly Milner Halls, August 12, 2008.

ARTICLES

"Animals Looted from Baghdad Zoo." BBC, April 17, 2003.

"Baghdad Lions Getting Ready to Go Home." BBC, June 1, 2003.

"Baghdad Lions to Roam Free in South Africa." BBC, May 24, 2003.

"Baghdad Zoo Animals Get Fed." BBC, April 20, 2003.

Bancroft, Colette. "Dogs and Big Cats Living Together." *St. Petersburg Times*, June 1, 2003.

Brand, William. "Bay Area Man Risks Life for Iraq Zoo Animals." *The Oakland Tribune*, June 10, 2003.

Cohen, Roger. "The Ghost in the Baghdad Museum." *The New York Times*, April 2, 2006.

DeYoanna, Michael. "Personal Space: Zoo Crew." *Colorado Springs Independent*, January 20, 2005.

Fisher, Ian. "WildAid Efforts at the Baghdad Zoo." *The New York Times*, May 5, 2003.

———. "Aftereffects: Baghdad Zookeepers' New Task: Getting Animals Back." *The New York Times*, May 6, 2003.

Garamone, Jim. "Baghdad Zoo Trip Tells CENTCOM Enlisted Leaders Volumes." American Forces Press Service, August 3, 2007.

Garen, Micah. "St. Francis of Baghdad." *Baghdad Bulletin*, June 4, 2003.

Gillespie, Tom. "Caring Kind: Iraqi Vet Continues Work in States." *The Pilot*, April 3, 2005.

Guthrie, Julian. "San Francisco Group Joins Effort to Save Baghdad Zoo Animals." *San Francisco Chronicle*, June 1, 2003.

Jones, Kenneth, "L.A.'s Douglas Will Premiere Bengal Tiger . . ." *Playbill News,* May 28, 2008.

"Keepers Go Back to Baghdad Zoo." BBC, May 5, 2003.

Keilman, John. "A Dog of War Comes Home." *Chicago Tribune*, April 23, 2003.

Kim, Kap. "Baghdad Zoo Opens Bear Habitat." *Black Anthem Military News*, November 7, 2007.

———. "Baghdad Zoo Opens New Horse Stable." American Forces Press Service, December 4, 2007.

Keys, Kathi. "Baghdad Zoo Gets New Life." *North Carolina Courier-Tribune*, January 6, 2005.

"Lions Eat Donkeys to Survive Hard Times at Baghdad Zoo." *Utusan Express*, May 8, 2003.

Orosz, Monica. "Group Honors Guardsman for Saving Animals Left to Die at Baghdad Zoos." *Charleston Daily Mail*, May 29, 2007.

Peake, Tracey. "Rebuilding a Zoo—from 6,000 Miles Away." NCSC News Service, January 29, 2008.

Raygoza, Geraldo. "Baghdad Amusement Park Lets the Bad Out of the Bag." *New University Magazine*, May 12, 2008.

Rickert, Mark S. "Soldiers Confiscate Neglected Petting Zoo Animals." *Defend America*, April 2003.

Russell, Rosalind. "Nothing Stops Baghdad Zoo Looters Except Lions." Reuters News Service, April 17, 2003.

Shaffer, Josh. "Tar Heel Tigers Will Help Repopulate Baghdad Zoo." *The News & Observer*, July 26, 2008.

Simmons, Ann M. "In Baghdad, a Sanctuary Restored." *Los Angeles Times,* December 30, 2007.

"Soldier Sparks Food Drive for Starving Iraqi Police Dogs." *USA Today*, January 7, 2005.

"Uday's Pet Lions Find New Home in Baghdad Zoo." AFP, July 28, 2003.

"USFWS Should Squelch Plan to Send US Tigers to Baghdad Zoo." PETA press release, July 26, 2008.

"US Troops Kill Baghdad Lions." BBC, April 22, 2003.

Wilkerson, Chad. "Army Veterinarian Treats Ailing Bear at Baghdad Zoo." *Defend America*, November 12, 2003.

Yates, Dean. "A Year On, Baghdad Zoo Faces Uncertain Future." Reuters News Service, July 25, 2004.

TV/RADIO

"Author Describes Rescue of Baghdad Zoo Animals." NPR *Talk of the Nation*, March 7, 2007.

"Baghdad Zoo Is Making a Comeback." MSNBC, April 25, 2008.

Holmes, Michael. "Baghdad Zoo: A Different Battle." CNN, April 17, 2003.

"Rescuing the Baghdad Zoo." CBS, April 29, 2008.

BOOKS

Anthony, Lawrence. *Babylon's Ark: The Incredible Wartime Rescue of the Baghdad Zoo.* New York: Thomas Dunne Books, 2007.

Vaughan, Brian K. *Pride of Baghdad.* New York: Vertigo/DC, 2006.

WEBSITES

IFAW
www.ifaw.org

Iraq Museum International
www.baghdadmuseum.org

After my tour ended in 2004, Dr. Farah Murrani and Brendan Whittington-Jones stayed for a considerable amount of time before they, too, left the country. Since then the zoo has been helped by dedicated people such as Sergeant First Class Robert Bussell and Sergeant First Class Herbert Mowery, who both continued to work at the zoo during their respective deployments and make improvements wherever possible. Although the initial campaign to save the zoo was a collective effort, I would like to offer my personal thanks to the following people who made significant contributions during my time there. There were many more people who all helped us in their own way, and although I cannot thank them all, the continued success of the Baghdad Zoo is a testament to their efforts.

Lawrence Anthony. Lawrence is a giant of a man, in both spirit and personality. Even before I met him, I had heard stories from the Iraqis about the man who traveled from South Africa to help the zoo. When we finally met, after days of near misses, I was not disappointed. Lawrence was a hard-to-deny force of will, determined to get things done despite the obstacles placed in front of him. He committed himself entirely to the effort and started the zoo down the road to recovery. Although Lawrence was only there during the initial months of the crisis, his personality left an indelible mark upon the zoo, its staff, and those people who helped in the recovery. His time there will never be forgotten, and his example will carry through the years to come.

Dr. Farah Murrani. Dr. Murrani came to us in the opening days of the recovery effort. Initially, her knowledge of various languages helped us bridge the language gap with the Iraqi staff. She later became a driving force at the zoo, served as the assistant zoo director, and was the administrator of the Iraqi Society for Animal Welfare. She and her family endured a tremendous amount of hardship during my time there, but she never stopped working to make the zoo a better place, for both the staff and the animals. She became, and still is, a lifelong friend.

Brendan Whittington-Jones. Brendan first showed up at the zoo in his Thula Thula Game Reserve uniform, carrying a much-needed tranquilizer gun. We have been friends ever since. Brendan represents the enduring adventurous spirit, willing to take on any task regardless of the difficulty or danger associated with it. He operated on lions, planned and constructed new animal enclosures, and personally managed funding, staff, and numerous other tasks. He was one of the key individuals who made the success of the zoo a reality, and without him, the recovery would have failed. Brendan is also an absolute rubbish cricket player with a disturbing affection for U.S. Army MREs.

Dr. Adel Salman Mousa. He risked his life working with us at the zoo and devoted himself completely to its recovery. His leadership was an example to the Iraqis and served daily to bolster the recovery efforts.

Dr. Wasseem Wali. He is an incredible person and helped in all of the thankless jobs that kept the animals healthy. He is still at the zoo today and continues to dedicate himself to the well-being of the animals that call the zoo home.

Saad, Ahmed, Akrum, Ali, Jaboori, and Salman. These were the staff of the zoo that came to work each day despite the death threats, the attacks, and the inherent danger of working with the Americans. Saad was beaten and stabbed in the skull by relatives for his efforts. Salman was killed by a car bomb. Their courage still serves as an example for me.

Colonel John Huntley, U.S. Army veterinarian and commander of the 414th Civil Affairs Battalion. He provided expert medical care and advice, as well as a stockpile of rye for our horses.

Colonel Mark Gants. He is an extremely talented man and led several medical operations and contributed to the education of the zoo's Iraqi staff.

Lieutenant Colonel Jose Lozada, U.S. Army veterinarian, 490th Civil Affairs Battalion. Dr. Lozada brought in more than fifty thousand dollars' worth of medicine and equipment for our animals, provided much needed medical support, and helped shave Lumpy of his matted fur . . . for which Lumpy was eternally grateful.

Specialist Erin McLoughlin. She provided day-to-day care for the animals and was critical in identifying the source of a disease that swept through the animal population of the zoo. She is, by far, the best veterinary technician I have ever met, and I am proud to have served with her.

Stephan Bognar. Perhaps the hardest-working man I have ever met in my life. He showed up at the gate with a single change of clothes and spent the next few months scrubbing cages, locating food, and helping us rebuild the zoo from the ground up. We couldn't have done it without him.

Dr. Barbara Maas. An intensely passionate animal conservationist who showed up with a truckful of food and saved the day when things were looking rough. Her intensity and fervor made an impression on us all.

Dr. David Jones, director of the North Carolina Zoo. He provided us with valuable insight and funding that allowed us to move from the crisis stage to long-term recovery planning and care of the animals.

Mariette Hopley and Jackson Zee. These two individuals represent the best side of people. They came to the zoo, contributed all that they had, and helped us achieve the impossible.

Captain Mark St. Laurent, 354th Civil Affairs Brigade and money man/comic relief. Mark provided the official funding to pay the staff of the zoo and helped us locate additional funding throughout the remaining year we were there. He also provided medical support to us, kept up our spirits when things looked bleak, and made one heck of a pizza from the care packages we were sent.

Specialist Martin, 354th Civil Affairs Brigade, who spent a large amount of his deployment to Iraq scraping animal dung from the back of his truck.

Engineers of 3rd Infantry Division who were stationed in al-Zawra Park during the initial invasion. I wish I could commend each and every one of them for their efforts. During the critical opening days, they were the soldiers who made the rest of this possible. If it were not for them, the zoo and its animals would have ceased to exist.

—William Sumner